Speaking Our Minds

Speaking Our Minds

SAGE ADVICE FROM SASSY WOMEN

Illustrated by Shawn Banner

ARIEL BOOKS

Andrews McMeel Publishing

Kansas City

www.andrewsmcmeel.com

ISBN: 0-8362-6812-1
Library of Congress Catalog Card Number: 98-84245

CONTENTS

INTRODUCTION

Women have always been masters of studying the world around them and reflecting on what they see. Their observations have a way of getting to the heart of things—often with a *zing* that makes us laugh out loud. Whether reflecting on work,

marriage, children, sex, politics, or life in general, their insights are like a delectable sauce which has been boiled down to its essence.

And how good it is to be able to laugh at what goes on around us! Humor has a way of helping us keep everything in perspective. If we can continue to smile while dealing with the constant complications of life, we will always be ahead of the game.

Women also know the importance of learning from one another. We grow from taking guidance and instruction from those who have been there before us. The quotations gathered here contain nuggets of wisdom that can help each of us on our way with new insights— and with a lighter heart.

WIT

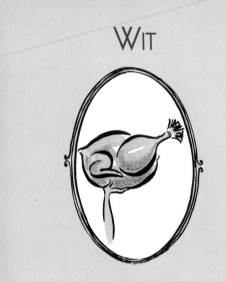

Never eat more than you can lift.
—*Miss Piggy*

*D*on't get your knickers in a knot.
Nothing is solved and it just makes
you walk funny.

—*Kathryn Carpenter*

When faced with a decision, I always ask,
"What would be the most fun?"

—*Peggy Walker*

Ask your child what he wants for dinner only if he's buying.

—*Fran Lebowitz*

Everyone's entitled to my opinion.

—*Madonna*

It's the good girls who keep the diaries;
the bad girls never have the time.

—*Tallulah Bankhead*

*I*f you haven't got anything nice to say about anyone, come and sit by me.

—*Alice Roosevelt Longworth*

I've been on a constant diet for the last two decades. I've lost a total of 789 pounds. By all accounts, I should be hanging from a charm bracelet.

—*Erma Bombeck*

He who hesitates is last.

—*Mae West*

*I*t doesn't matter what you do in the bedroom as long as you don't do it in the street and frighten the horses.

—*Mrs. Patrick Campbell*

I've been on a calendar, but never on time.

—*Marilyn Monroe*

Cleaning your house while your kids are still growing is like shoveling your walk before it stops snowing.

—*Phyllis Diller*

17

Too much
of a good
thing can be
wonderful.

—Mae West

Whenever one of us falls in love,
our friends watch as they would the
progress of a disease.

—*Ellen Gilchrist*

I never know how much of what I say is true.

—*Bette Midler*

Housework can't kill you, but why take a
chance?

—*Phyllis Diller*

What you eat standing up doesn't count.

—*Beth Barnes*

There are three ways to get something done;
do it yourself, hire someone, or forbid your
kids to do it.

—*Monta Crane*

WISDOM

Arrange whatever pieces come your way.
—*Virginia Woolf*

I have always preferred having wings to having things.

—*Patricia Schroeder*

It is better to light a candle than to curse the darkness.

—*Eleanor Roosevelt*

To keep a lamp burning we have to keep putting oil in it.

—*Mother Teresa*

*T*here is no pleasure in having nothing to do; the fun is having lots to do and not doing it.

—*Mary Little*

General notions are generally wrong.

—*Lady Mary Wortley Montagu*

*T*hey sicken of the calm, who knew the storm.

—*Dorothy Parker*

The trouble with being in the rat race is that even if you win, you're still a rat.

—*Lily Tomlin*

Groan and forget it.

—*Jessamyn West*

29

*I*f you are all wrapped up in yourself, you are overdressed.

—*Kate Halverson*

If only we'd stop trying to be happy, we could have a pretty good time.

—*Edith Wharton*

Don't be afraid that your life will end. Be afraid that it will never begin.

—*Grace Hansen*

30

*F*ond as we are of our loved ones, there comes at times during their absence an unexplained peace.

—*Anne Shaw*

People change and forget to tell each other.

—*Lillian Hellman*

We thought we were running away from the grown-ups, and now we are the grown-ups.

—*Margaret Atwood*

I think, at a child's birth, if a mother could ask a fairy godmother to endow it with the most useful gift, that gift should be curiosity.

—*Eleanor Roosevelt*

Always be smarter than the people who hire you.

—*Lena Horne*

To think too long about doing a thing often becomes its undoing.

—*Eva Young*

I have found that sitting in a place
where you have never sat before can
be inspiring.

—*Dodie Smith*

Give to the world the best that you have,
and the best will come back to you.

—*Madeline Bridge*

Some people think they are worth a lot of
money just because they have it.

—*Fannie Hurst*

*I*f you look at life one way,
there is always cause for alarm.
—*Elizabeth Bowen*

38

MEN

Macho does not prove mucho.
—Zsa Zsa Gabor

*T*he trouble with some women is that they get all excited about nothing—and then marry him.

—*Cher*

When Harvard men say they have graduated from Radcliffe, then we've made it.

—*Jacqueline Kennedy Onassis*

Women want mediocre men, and men are working hard to be as mediocre as possible.

—*Margaret Mead*

41

*I*f you want anything said, ask a man. If you
want anything done, ask a woman.

—*Margaret Thatcher*

*T*he male is a domestic animal which, if treated with firmness and kindness, can be trained to do most things.

—*Jilly Cooper*

Behind every great man there is a surprised woman.

—*Maryon Pearson*

*H*usbands are like fires. They go out when unattended.

—Zsa Zsa Gabor

A successful man is one who makes more money than his wife can spend. A successful woman is one who can find such a man.

—*Lana Turner*

Giving a man space is like giving a dog a computer: Chances are he will not use it wisely.

—*Bette-Jane Raphael*

*B*efore marriage, a man declares he would lay down his life to serve you; after marriage, he won't even lay down his paper to talk to you.

—Helen Rowland

Sometimes I wonder if men and women really suit each other. Perhaps they should live next door and just visit now and then.

—*Katharine Hepburn*

I have yet to hear a man ask for advice on how to combine marriage and a career.

—*Gloria Steinem*

W hen a girl marries she exchanges
the attentions of many men . . .

. . . for the inattention of one.

—*Helen Rowland*

WOMEN

I don't have the time every day to put on makeup. I need that time to clean my rifle.
—*Henriette Mantel*

Whatever women do they must do twice as well as men to be thought half as good. Luckily, this is not difficult.

—*Charlotte Whitton*

After thirty, a body has a mind of its own.

—*Bette Midler*

I buried a lot of my ironing in the backyard.

—*Phyllis Diller*

I would venture to guess that Anon, who wrote so many poems without signing them, was often a woman.

—*Virginia Woolf*

53

*P*lain women know more about men than beautiful ones do.

—*Katharine Hepburn*

The people I'm furious with are the women's liberationists. They keep getting up on soapboxes and proclaiming that women are brighter than men. It's true but it should be kept quiet or it ruins the whole racket.

—*Anita Loos*

I hate housework! You make the beds, you do the dishes—and six months later you have to start all over again.

—*Joan Rivers*

54

I want to feel myself part of things, of the great drift and swirl, not cut off, missing things, like being sent to bed early as a child.

—*Joanna Field*

In love with her own husband? Monstrous! What a selfish woman!

—*Jennie Jerome Churchill*

Men are taught to apologize for their weaknesses, women for their strengths.

—*Lois Wyse*

Some of us are becoming the men we wanted to marry.

—*Gloria Steinem*

*T*he real menace in dealing with a five-year-old is that in no time at all you begin to sound like a five-year-old.

—*Jean Kerr*

Women want men, careers, money, children, friends, luxury, comfort, independence, freedom, respect, love, and a three-dollar panty hose that won't run.

—*Phyllis Diller*

Women who aspire to be as good as men lack ambition.

—*Graffiti*

*W*hy dust the house when you can just wait a couple of years and get a snowblower?

—*Unknown*

Woman's place is in the House and in the Senate.

—*Gloria Schaeffer*

Do not compare yourself with others, for you are a unique and wonderful creation. Make your own beautiful footprints in the snow.

—*Barbara Kimball*

*R*emember, Ginger Rogers did everything Fred Astaire did, but she did it backwards and in high heels.

—*Faith Whittlesey*

LIFE

Earth's crammed with heaven.
—*Elizabeth Barrett Browning*

*I*t's never too late to be what you might
have been.

—*George Eliot*

She didn't know it couldn't be done so she
went ahead and did it.

—*Mary's Almanac*

I succeeded by saying what everyone else is
thinking.

—*Joan Rivers*

We are all in this together—by ourselves.

—*Lily Tomlin*

*A*m I like the optimist who, while falling ten stories from a building, says at each story, "I'm all right so far"?

—*Gretel Ehrlich*

Those who do not know how to weep with their whole heart don't know how to laugh either.

—*Golda Meir*

Fill what's empty. Empty what's full. Scratch where it itches.

—*Alice Roosevelt Longworth*

I think, therefore I'm single.

—*Liz Winston*

What I wanted to be when I grew up was—in charge.

—*Wilma Vaught*

Nobody can make you feel inferior without your consent.

—*Eleanor Roosevelt*

If I had to live my life again I'd make all the same mistakes, only sooner.

—*Tallulah Bankhead*

68

*T*he way I see it, if you want the rainbow, you gotta put up with the rain.

—*Dolly Parton*

Ninety-eight percent of the adults in this country are decent, hardworking, honest Americans. It's the other lousy 2 percent that gets all the publicity. But then—we elected them.

—*Lily Tomlin*

What you have become is the price you paid to get what you used to want.

—*Mignon McLaughlin*

*I*f you think you can, you can.
And if you think you can't,
you're right.

—*Mary Kay Ash*

I'd like to grow very old as slowly
as possible.

—Irene Mayer Selznick

As time passes, we all get better at blazing a trail through the thicket of advice.

—*Margot Bennett*

Standing in the middle of the road is very dangerous; you get knocked down by traffic from both sides.

—*Margaret Thatcher*

Y ou may be disappointed if you fail, but you are doomed if you don't try.

—*Beverly Sills*

I never intended to become a run-of-the-mill person.

—*Barbara Jordan*

When I look into the future, it's so bright it burns my eyes.

—*Oprah Winfrey*

Striving for excellence motivates you. Striving for perfection is demoralizing.

—*Dr. Harriet Braiker*

I wanted a perfect ending. . . . Now I've learned, the hard way, that some poems don't rhyme, and some stories don't have a clear beginning, middle, and end. Life is about not knowing, having to change, taking the moment and making the best of it, without knowing what's going to happen next. Delicious ambiguity.

—*Gilda Radner*

If we could sell our experiences for what they cost us we'd be millionaires.

—*Abigail Van Buren*

My husband and I have figured out a really good system about the house-work: Neither one of us does it.

—*Dottie Archibald*

This book was typeset in Kabel Book and

Stempel Schneidler Medium Italic by

Ann Obringer of BTD in NYC.